W9-BCK-923

BABY'S IN BLACK

My thanks for their help, time and patience go to Astrid, Ulf, Micha, Sascha and Jan-Frederik – and above all to Line and Matti: you know what for.

Translated from the German by Michael Waaler

Published by First Second
First Second is an imprint of Roaring Brook Press, a division of Holtzbrinck Publishing Holdings Limited Partnership
175 Fifth Avenue, New York, New York 10010

Originally published in Germany by Reprodukt under the title *Baby's in Black: The Story of Astrid Kirchherr & Stuart Sutcliffe* (2010)

Cataloging-in-Publication Data is on file at the Library of Congress

ISBN 978-1-59643-771-5

First Second books are available for special promotions and premiums.
For details, contact: Director of Special Markets, Holtzbrinck Publishers.

First American edition 2012
Book design by Colleen AF Venable
Printed in the United States of America

10 9 8 7 6 5 4 3 2 1

Arne Bellstorf

BABY'S IN BLACK

Astrid Kirchherr, Stuart Sutcliffe, and The Beatles

:01
First Second
New York & London

»Grosse Freiheit«

October 1960

RINNG

RRRING
RRIING
RRINNG
RRING

KLAUS?

YOU WON'T BELIEVE WHERE I'VE JUST COME FROM!

ARE YOU CRAZY? DO YOU KNOW HOW LATE IT IS?

NO, I ...
SSSHH!

MY MOTHER'S SLEEPING. COME INTO THE KITCHEN.

I HAVE TO TELL YOU WHERE I'VE BEEN.

LISTEN ...
... YOU'RE NOT STILL MAD, ARE YOU?

I DIDN'T KNOW WHERE I WAS GOING ... I JUST WANTED TIME TO THINK, ABOUT US. SO I WANDERED AROUND, UNTIL I FOUND MYSELF ON THE REEPERBAHN ...

Mehrer
REGINA
AB 4 UHR FRÜH
TABU
Regina
HOT
Spiel-
CASINO

I DIDN'T FEEL LIKE BEING AROUND ALL THOSE PEOPLE, BUT I WAS HUNGRY AND I WANTED TO GET SOME FRIES, SO I WENT ON UP TO THE CORNER OF GROSSE FREIHEIT.

THEN I KEPT ON WALKING ... PAST ALL THE DOORMEN DRAGGING PEOPLE INTO THEIR CLUBS. OCCASIONALLY I COULD SEE THROUGH THE DOORS TO WHAT WAS WAITING INSIDE ...

BIER

I REALLY DID WANT TO GO HOME, BUT THEN I HEARD THIS MUSIC COMING FROM A CELLAR ... IT WAS LIVE MUSIC ... AND IT WAS INCREDIBLE. IT WENT RIGHT THROUGH ME ...

I JUST HAD TO GO IN AND TAKE A LOOK ...
SOMEHOW, I MANAGED TO BUILD UP THE COURAGE
AND PUSHED PAST A BUNCH OF TOUGH-LOOKING GUYS,
INTO THE ENTRANCE.

COME ON OVER BABY ...

I SAID COME ON OVER BABY

BABY...
YOU CAN'T GO WRONG

COME ON OVER BABY...
SIT DOWN OR GET OUT.

... WHOLE LOTTA SHAK

YOU CAN'T GO WRONG ...

I DIDN'T WANT TO DRAW ANY MORE ATTENTION SO I STAYED PUT AT MY TABLE. I'D ALREADY COUNTED OUT THE CHANGE WHEN THE WAITER CAME WITH MY BEER. HE JUST NODDED WHEN I GAVE HIM A TIP ...

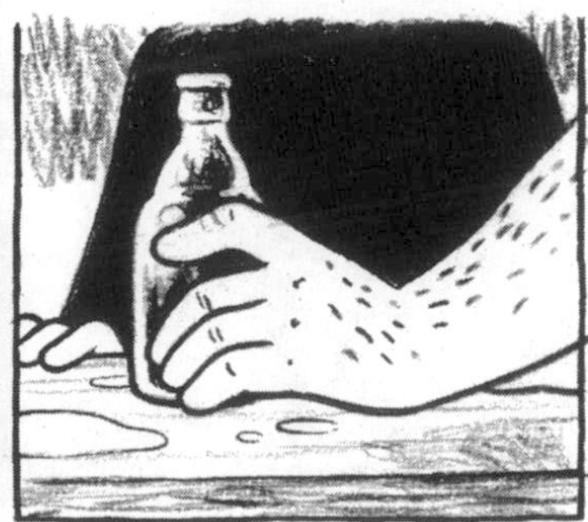

AFTER A BLOND GUY AS SKINNY AS A SKELETON FINISHED HIS SET, THE JUKEBOX CAME ON FOR A WHILE AND I COULD WATCH THE CROWD, UNDISTURBED. I HAD A GOOD VIEW FROM MY TABLE.

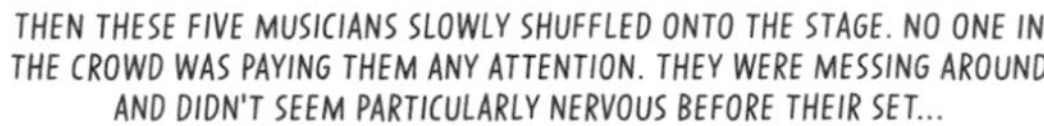

THEY WERE ALL DRESSED THE SAME, IN CHEAP JACKETS, TIGHT FLANNEL TROUSERS, AND HIGH, POINTY BUCKLED SHOES. THEY LOOKED VERY ODD.

THE BASSIST MADE ME THINK OF JAMES DEAN. HE WORE DARK SUNGLASSES THE WHOLE TIME AND STOOD COMPLETELY STILL ON STAGE.

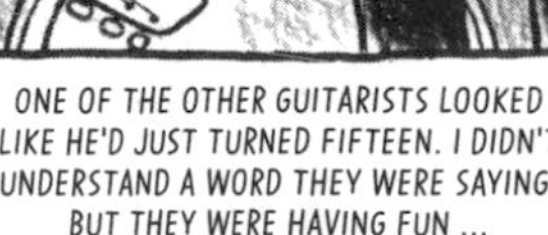

FOR GOODNESS SAKE, I'VE GOT THE HIPPY HIPPY SHAKE

I'VE GOT THE SHAKE
OH THE HIPPY HIPPY SHAKE

OH, I CAN'T KEEP STILL
WITH THE HIPPY HIPPY SHAKE

OOH ... THE HIPPY HIPPY SHAKE

EVERYONE STARTED DANCING AND I DRIFTED TOWARD THE STAGE. IT WAS INCREDIBLE ... THE ATMOSPHERE. IT FELT LIKE THE ENTIRE ROOM WAS MOVING TO THE RHYTHM OF THE MUSIC.

THEY PLAYED ONE SONG AFTER ANOTHER WITHOUT STOPPING. THE SINGER WITH QUIVERING NOSTRILS GOT LOUDER AND LOUDER AND WAS SCREAMING HIS HEART OUT ...

ONE OF THEM WAS SO HYPED UP HE WAS BOUNCING UP AND DOWN LIKE A RUBBER BALL ... BOUNCING UP TO THE CEILING, LIKE HE WAS ON A TRAMPOLINE. HE DID THE SPILTS IN THE AIR ... WHILE PLAYING HIS GUITAR!

I STOOD THERE DRENCHED IN SWEAT, SPEECHLESS BUT HAPPY. I'D FORGOTTEN EVERYTHING AROUND ME ...

I THOUGHT ABOUT STAYING TO SEE THE NEXT BAND, BUT THEN I TOOK OFF BECAUSE I JUST HAD TO COME HERE AND TELL YOU ABOUT IT.

YEAH, I KNOW WHAT YOU'RE THINKING ... ST. PAULI'S A ROUGH NEIGHBORHOOD, BUT ...
ASTRID, YOU'VE JUST GOTTA SEE THIS!

THEY PLAY THERE EVERY NIGHT. THE WHOLE NIGHT LONG.
ONCE YOU'VE BEEN THERE AND SEEN IT FOR YOURSELF...

I'VE NEVER SEEN YOU SO EXCITED ABOUT ANYTHING LIKE THIS BEFORE.

THAT MEANS YOU'LL COME WITH ME TOMORROW NIGHT?

I DIDN'T SAY THAT.
BUT I'LL THINK ABOUT IT.

WELL, WHATEVER. I'M DEFINITELY GOING BACK.

THE FIRST TIME I WAS ON THE REEPERBAHN WAS WITH THEO ...
IT WAS PRETTY MUCH THE LAST TIME, TOO.

I FOUND IT A LITTLE SCARY ...
I THINK I WAS FIFTEEN.

THEN IT'S TIME YOU WENT BACK AGAIN.

I PROMISE YOU, YOU WON'T REGRET IT.

YEAH.
THAT'S GOOD.
I PREFER THE
FRAMING HERE,
TOO.
TOMORROW,
CAN YOU MAKE
ANOTHER TWO PRINTS
IN THIS FORMAT?
YES,
OF COURSE.

ARE YOU COMING AFTER WORK?

IT'S THE LAST SHOWING OF *LES ENFANTS DU PARADIS*.
PIERRO AND HIS BOYFRIEND REALLY WANT TO SEE IT AGAIN.

YEAH, I'D LIKE TO ...
BUT I PROMISED TO GO OUT WITH KLAUS.

KLAUS? ARE YOU TWO ...
... EVEN STILL TOGETHER?

NO. WE'RE TOO ... DIFFERENT. IN MY OPINION.

HUH. AND I THOUGHT HE WAS BECOMING MORE AND MORE LIKE YOU.
BUT HE'S NOT REALLY WHAT YOU THOUGHT HE WAS, IS HE?

ANKER Bar
Hans Karl
ELBSCHLOSS BIER

THIS IS THE FIRST TIME I'VE EVER BEEN ABLE TO TALK YOU INTO ANYTHING.

YEAH. IT'S ALWAYS BEEN THE OTHER WAY AROUND ... BUT THIS TIME YOU'VE REALLY MADE ME CURIOUS.

IT'S THERE ON THE CORNER.

SERKELLER
HAMBURG - ST. PAULI
der Rock'n Roll FANS
OBER-NOVEMBER-DEZEMBER
ORIGINAL
HIS HURICAN
ENGLAND-LIVERPOOL
RORY STORM?
... AND THE BEATLES. THAT'S THEM!

I THINK RORY STORM'S ALWAYS ON FIRST.
THEN THEY TAKE TURNS PLAYING.

OH ... HELLO!

THE SAFEST
PLACE IS UP FRONT
NEXT TO THE STAGE,
AT THAT TABLE,
THERE.

AH, HERE
COMES THE FIRST
BAND ...

THE BEST THINGS IN LIFE ARE FREE...

BUT YOU CAN KEEP 'EM FOR THE BIRDS AND BEES...

NOW GIVE ME MONEY...

THAT'S WHAT I WANT...

HA HA
HA HA HA
COME ON! LET'S GET RIGHT UP BY THE STAGE!

JUST WAIT UNTIL YOU SEE THE LITTLE ONE – GEORGE!

GEORGE? I LIKE JOHN THE BEST!
LOOK! THERE'S PAUL!

GOOD EVENING, LADIES AND GENTLEMEN ... WELCOME TO THE KAISERKELLER!

YOU MAKE ME DIZZY MISS LIZZY

YOU MAKE ME DIZZY MISS LIZZY ... WHEN YOU DO THE STROLL

COME ON, MISS LIZZY ... LOVE ME 'FORE I GROW TOO OLD

COME ON, GIVE ME FEVER

PUT YOUR LITTLE HAND IN MINE

YOU MAKE ME DIZZY MISS LIZZY... OH GIRL, YOU LOOK SO FINE

A-ROCKIN' AND A-ROLLIN'

GIRL I SAID I WISH YOU WERE MINE

YOU MAKE ME DIZZY MISS LIZZY

... WHEN YOU CALL MY NAME

O-O-OH OH BABY ...

SAY YOU'RE DRIVING ME INSANE

NOT QUITE.

HE'S MUCH BETTER LOOKING THAN JAMES DEAN.

HE'S GOT SOMETHING ... SOMETHING DIFFERENT FROM THE OTHERS ...

I JUST WISH HE'D TAKE OFF THOSE SUNGLASSES.

»My favorite color«

ASTRID, ARE YOU GOING TO THAT JAZZ CLUB IN THE COLONNADE AGAIN?

NO, WE'RE GOING TO ST. PAULI.
KLAUS FOUND AN ENGLISH BAND THERE ...

ST. PAULI? I HAD NO IDEA ...

OKAY, I KNOW I'M A LITTLE OUT OF TOUCH, BUT WHAT KIND OF CONCERT IS THIS, EXACTLY?

DON'T WORRY. I'M NOT GOING ALONE.

Marika
RÖKK

... BUT THAT'S A GREAT WAY TO GET TO TALK TO THEM.
WE'LL SEE. I'LL GIVE IT A TRY.

I DUNNO HOW YOU KEEP IT UP.
YOU SPEND EVERY NIGHT IN THAT CELLAR UNTIL DAWN ...

... AND THEN AT EIGHT O'CLOCK YOU GO BACK TO WORK.

IT'S BEEN LIKE THAT FOR ALMOST TWO WEEKS NOW.
WELL, WHEN I GET HOME FROM WORK I TRY TO SLEEP A LITTLE BEFORE I GO OUT AGAIN.
I DON'T THINK HE CAN KEEP IT UP MUCH LONGER.

YEAH, WELL ... APART FROM ASTRID, I HAVEN'T BEEN ABLE TO GET ANYONE ELSE TO COME WITH ME.

I'M NOT SURPRISED! I DON'T KNOW ANYONE BRAVE ENOUGH TO GO TO A BAR LIKE THAT.

YEAH, ESPECIALLY DURING THE WEEK ...

... A DINGY BAR FULL OF HOOLIGANS, SAILORS, AND TROUBLEMAKERS.

YEAH, WE AIN'T FAKIN' ...

WHOLE LOTTA SHAKIN GOIN' ON

I JUST CAN'T BELIEVE IT.
IT'S THE LAST PLACE I'D EVER EXPECT TO SEE KLAUS AND ASTRID.

IT'S JUST NOT THEIR WORLD. DURING THE DAY ASTRID WOULD GO OUT OF HER WAY TO AVOID THE PEOPLE IN HERE ...

... THANK YOU AND GOOD NIGHT!
AND DON'T FORGET: WE WON THE WAR!
CLAP
CLAP

IT'S INCREDIBLE THAT KLAUS WAS EVER BRAVE ENOUGH TO COME IN HERE ...

I DUNNO. AS LONG AS YOU KEEP TO YOURSELF, NO ONE BOTHERS YOU.
I'M NOT WORRIED AND KLAUS SEEMS TO GET ALONG WITH THE STAFF. THEY KEEP AN EYE ON HIM.

MAYBE THEY'D LIKE MORE CUSTOMERS LIKE US ...
WE DON'T MAKE TROUBLE, WE PAY FOR OUR DRINKS, AND WE TIP WELL.

I'M JUST STAYING FOR ONE MORE COKE, KLAUS.

SO HOW'S IT GOING? HAVE YOU SPOKEN TO THE BEATLES YET?

NO. NOT YET.

HE'S BEEN WAITING FOR THE RIGHT MOMENT THE WHOLE NIGHT.

GO ON. GO OVER ... ONE OF THEM IS SITTING BY HIMSELF ON THE EDGE OF THE STAGE.

JOHN?

WHAT?

I'VE ... I'VE DESIGNED AN ALBUM COVER.
I THOUGHT ... MAYBE YOU MIGHT WANT TO SEE IT?
WALK DON'T RUN

OH RIGHT. YOU'RE BETTER OFF SHOWING STUART SUMMAT LIKE THAT. HE'S OUR RESIDENT ARTIST.

STU!
TAKE A LOOK AT THIS, MATE.

NOW HE'S TALKING TO THE BASSIST ...

LOOK, HE'S FINALLY TAKEN THOSE SUNGLASSES OFF.

THIS IS GABI ... AND ASTRID.

PLEASED TO MEET YOU.

PLEASE ... JOIN US.
I'LL GO AND GET SOME DRINKS.

OH, AND THIS HERE'S JOHN.

YOU GIRLS ARE HERE ALMOST EVERY NIGHT, RIGHT? I RECOGNIZE YOU BECAUSE ...

WELL, YOU DON'T LOOK LIKE THE USUAL CROWD THAT COMES HERE.

AND YOU'RE THE ONLY ONES WHO APPLAUD AT THE END OF EVERY SONG ...
FRIENDLY GERMANS TAKE SOME GETTIN' USED TO, YOU KNOW.

DOES SHE EVEN UNDERSTAND A WORD THEY'RE SAYING? ASTRID CAN BARELY SPEAK ENGLISH.

AH, THAT DOESN'T MATTER!
IT'LL BE ALL RIGHT SOMEHOW.

HEY, PAUL!
YOU EVER SEEN SUCH A STRANGE BUNCH OF GERMANS?
NAH ... I THOUGHT YOU WERE ALL FRENCH.

THAT'S RIGHT! YOU LOOK LIKE THOSE ...THOSE EXISTENTIALISTS.
I GUESS YOU'VE READ ALL THAT SARTRE AND CAMUS AND ALL THAT STUFF ...

OH, WE JUST LOVE EVERYTHING FRENCH ...
IT'S NOT ONLY FRENCH LITERATURE AND PHILOSOPHY.

IT'S THE MUSIC, THE PAINTERS, POETS, FILMS, ANYTHING ...

DO YOU KNOW JEAN COCTEAU? HIS WORK IS REALLY INSPIRING.

AND WHERE DID YOU GET THEM BLACK TURTLENECKS?

THEY GOTTA BE FRENCH, RIGHT?

YES, I BOUGHT THIS ONE AT THE FLEA MARKET IN PARIS.

AND DID YOU GET YOUR HAIR CUT THERE?

NO. ASTRID CUT MY HAIR.

FUNNY LOOKING, ISN'T IT, GEORGE?

WOULD SUIT PAUL, THOUGH ...
HA, HA! JUST A SEC!

JA, JA, MEIN FÜHRER! HAIL HITLER!

HA HA
HA HA

HA HA
HA HA

WELL, THEY'RE DEFINITELY NOT LIKE I THOUGHT THEY'D BE ...
YEAH, BUT I LIKE THEM.

I MEAN, WOULD YOU HAVE EVER GUESSED THAT JOHN AND STUART STUDIED ART?
AS I UNDERSTOOD IT, STUART'S ONLY BEEN IN THE BAND A SHORT TIME. THEY MET IN COLLEGE.

I COULD TALK ABOUT ANYTHING WITH STUART. I MEAN, AS MUCH AS MY ENGLISH ALLOWS.

BUT AS SOON AS HE STARTS TALKING TO JOHN I CAN'T KEEP UP ANY MORE.
YEAH, HE AND JOHN SEEM CLOSE.

WHEN THEY TALK TO EACH OTHER, I DON'T UNDERSTAND A WORD.
BUT I DON'T THINK IT'S JUST BECAUSE OF MY ENGLISH. THEY SHARE THEIR OWN SPECIAL HUMOR ...

DID YOU CATCH WHERE THEY LIVE? IT'S IN A BACK ROOM IN THE BAMBI CINEMA ...
JOHN WAS COMPLAINING ABOUT THE GUY WHO RUNS THE KAISERKELLER. IT SOUNDS LIKE HE DOESN'T TREAT THEM VERY WELL.
AND POOR LITTLE GEORGE ... HE'S ONLY SEVENTEEN!
HE'S NOT EVEN ALLOWED TO BE THERE AFTER TEN O'CLOCK ...
PHEW ... I'M SO TIRED I CAN BARELY WALK. MAYBE I SHOULD STAY HOME TOMORROW.
YEAH, I'M TIRED TOO. BUT I DON'T THINK I'LL GET TO SLEEP EASILY.

THAT'S HOW I'D LIKE TO DO IT ...
THIS IS A GOOD EXAMPLE.
DO YOU SEE WHAT I'M TALKING ABOUT? HOW HE USES LIGHT ...
YES. IT LOOKS GREAT.
I'D LIKE TO TRY IT AGAIN.
NOW, I HAVE THEM HERE SOMEWHERE ...
... YOU HAVE TO SEE THEM.
HIS PORTRAITS ARE UNSURPASSED.

THE LIGHTING IS THE MOST IMPORTANT ASPECT. THAT'S WHAT CREATES THE ATMOSPHERE.
YOU CAN SET IT UP ...
BUT, UNFORTUNATELY, THAT'S NOT ALL IT TAKES.
SEE THIS EXPRESSION HERE ... SOMETHING LIKE THAT IS DIFFICULT TO CAPTURE ON CAMERA.

I DON'T KNOW IF I CAN EXPLAIN IT. THEY'RE JUST EXACTLY WHAT I'VE BEEN LOOKING FOR ...
I HAVE TO PHOTOGRAPH THEM.

WHERE? AT REINHART'S STUDIO?

NO, THAT'S NOT THE RIGHT SETTING. IT HAS TO BE OUTSIDE.
I NEED A BACKGROUND THAT FITS THEM.

AND ... WHAT DO YOU THINK THAT IS?

FIRST, I WANT TO TAKE SOME GROUP PHOTOS OF THEM, AS THEY ARE.
WITH THEIR LEATHER JACKETS AND INSTRUMENTS ...

I ALREADY HAVE IT IN MY HEAD EXACTLY HOW IT SHOULD LOOK.

ANYWAY ...
I HAVE TO ASK
THEM, FIRST.
I THINK
YOU'RE GOING TO
HAVE TO HELP ME
THERE, KLAUS ...
OH,
I'M SURE
THEY'LL
THINK IT'S
GREAT.

I'VE ALREADY
TOLD THEM THAT
YOU'RE A FANTASTIC
PHOTOGRAPHER.

YEAH,
BUT I THINK ...
I MEAN,
I'D LIKE ...

I HAVE
TO BE ABLE
TO SPEAK TO THEM.
YOU HAVE TO HELP
ME IMPROVE MY
ENGLISH, OKAY?

Dujardin
Jmperial
Weinbrand
LEDER

KLAUS SAID SHE'S A PROFESSIONAL PHOTOGRAPHER ... YOU THINK SHE'LL SHOW UP ALONE?

THERE SHE IS.

AND SHE'S DRIVING!
I CAN'T BELIEVE IT ...
THAT'S A VOLKSWAGEN CONVERTIBLE ...

GOOD MORNING.

YOU'RE THE MOST AMAZING BIRD I'VE EVER MET, YOU KNOW?

LOOKS LIKE A FAIRGROUND. THERE'S A ROLLERCOASTER OVER THERE!
YEAH. WE SHOULD COME BACK WHEN THEY'VE OPENED THIS THING.

ALL RIGHT. SO, LIKE, WHAT DO YOU WANT US TO DO?
AND HOW DO WE LOOK? ... *WUNDERBAR?*

JA. YOU LOOK ... PERFECT.

PLEASE, GO OVER THERE ...
AND SIT WITH THE GUITAR ...

UM ... YOU WANT ME TO CLIMB UP ON THAT TRUCK?
HEY, GEORGE! STU! GET OVER HERE!
CLICK
GOOD ... LOOK HERE TO ME.
CLICK
CLICK
CLICK
THANK YOU VERY MUCH.

GOOD.
VERY GOOD ...

HUGO HAA

YEAH,
REALLY NICE
PHOTOS.

LOOK AT THE SIZE OF THE THING!
I'VE NEVER SEEN A PICTURE THIS BIG.
CHRIST! ME NEITHER.

JOHN, YOU'RE LOOKING DEAD GOOD IN THIS ONE.

YEAH AND ME!
GIVE A LOOK, WILL YA ...

I CAN'T BELIEVE IT'S US.

THEY'RE SIMPLY AMAZING, ASTRID.

I GET THE FEELING THEY LIKE THEM A LOT.

YOUR PHOTOS TURNED OUT REALLY GREAT. ESPECIALLY THE ONES ON THE TRUCK.
AND, WELL ... IT HAS TO BE SAID, YOUR SUBJECTS ARE VERY PHOTOGENIC.

YEAH. I'D LIKE TO DO SOME MORE PICTURES OF THEM.

I NEED SOME BREAKFAST.
LET'S GO TO HARALD'S.
HARALD?

YEAH ... I'M STARVING.
HARALD DOES THE BEST FRY-UP IN TOWN. HE'S EVEN GOT CORNFLAKES.

I CAN'T EAT BRATWURST AND KRAUT EVERY DAY.

YOUR PHOTOGRAPHS ARE GREAT. I REALLY LIKE THEM.

BIER
ELBSCH
OH ... THANK YOU.

WELL, THEY JUST NEEDED A BASS PLAYER ...
AND JOHN ASKED ME COZ HE KNOWS I LOVE ROCK 'N' ROLL.

I DUNNO ... I SAID YES, BOUGHT A BASS, AND NOW I'M HERE IN HAMBURG WITH THE GROUP.

AND YOU ... YOU LIKE IT?

HAMBURG?
I'M STARTING TO LIKE IT MORE.

GLP...
MPF

ASTRID, LOOK AT THAT ...

MPF ... WHAT ARE YOU LOOKING AT?
OH, NOTHING ...
ALL'S GOOD.
DON'T WORRY ABOUT JOHN. HE ALWAYS EATS LIKE AN ANIMAL WHEN HE'S TIRED AND HUNGRY.
I RECKON WE MUST BE THE BIGGEST BUNCH OF SCALLIES YOU'VE EVER BEEN OUT WITH ...
YES, MAYBE.
BUT ... I AM BEGINNING TO LIKE IT.

I DON'T KNOW. PETE HAD OTHER PLANS ...

BUT THEY'RE ALL STILL THRILLED BY YOUR PHOTOS, RIGHT?
YEAH, I THINK SO.

AND THEY WERE REALLY HAPPY ABOUT YOUR MASHED POTATOES WITH PEAS.
I THINK IT'S EXACTLY WHAT THEY WANTED.

KLAUS WENT TO VISIT THEM RECENTLY ... THEY'RE ALL SLEEPING IN A SMALL MOVIE THEATER, NEXT TO THE RESTROOMS.
IT'S HORRIBLE ... HE SAYS IT'S MORE LIKE A WINDOWLESS CELLAR ... AND NOW THAT IT'S GETTING COLD ...

AND THE ONLY PLACE THEY CAN WASH THEMSELVES IS IN THE PUBLIC TOILETS THERE.

IS THAT TEA YOU'VE MADE?
YES. WITH MILK AND SUGAR, RIGHT?

DANKE SCHOEN!
YOU'RE JUST TOO GOOD TO BE TRUE, ASTRID!

THAT WAS LIKE THE FIRST PROPER ENGLISH MEAL WE'VE HAD SINCE WE GOT TO HAMBURG.

I'M PLEASED THEY LIKED IT. TELL THEM I'D BE HAPPY TO COOK FOR THEM AGAIN ...
... AND THAT THEY CAN USE OUR BATHROOM ANY TIME THEY WANT.

AH! THAT HIT THE SPOT. YOU'RE A LIFESAVER, YOU KNOW THAT?

NICE PLACE ... WHAT'S THE TREE BRANCH FOR?
I PAINTED IT BLACK.

YOU'RE MAD, ASTRID. THERE'S LOADS OF BLACK IN HERE.

IT'S MY FAVORITE COLOR.

MINE IS RED.

Juliette Gréco
PHILIPS
ANYONE WANNA HEAR THIS JULIETTE GRECO RECORD?

NO ... BUT WHY DON'T YOU PUT ON THAT MOZART SYMPHONY AGAIN?
YEAH. I LIKED THAT.

KRRK
UM ... INTERESTING COLLECTION.

HAVEN'T YOU GOT ANY ROCK 'N' ROLL RECORDS?

ANY CHUCK BERRY OR LITTLE RICHARD?
NO.

ELVIS PRESLEY? BUDDY HOLLY?
NO.

I LOVE ELVIS. HE'S THE BEST AROUND.
I COULD BRING SOME OF HIS RECORDS WITH ME NEXT TIME.

I LIKE THE RHYTHM ... WHO'S THAT?

IT'S IGOR STRAVIN...SKY.
HM. I WANT TO ASK YOU IF ... I CAN ...

CAN I MAKE MORE PHOTOGRAPHS ...
... OF YOU?

YEAH, SURE. WE ALL LOVED YOUR PICTURES.
YOU WANNA GO TO THE FAIRGROUND AGAIN?

NO, NO ... SOMEWHERE ELSE. BY THE RIVER MAYBE, AND ...
... AND JUST YOU.

PLEASE ... DON'T TALK SO ... FAST.

OH, RIGHT ... WELL, THIS GUY EVEN BOUGHT THE PAINTING WHEN THE EXHIBITION WAS OVER.
IT WAS THE FIRST PAINTING I EVER SOLD.

I DEFINITELY WANNA START PAINTING AGAIN.

BUT YOU ... YOU WANT TO BE IN THE GROUP?
I MEAN ... YOU LIKE TO MAKE MUSIC AND ... PLAY WITH THE GROUP?
I LIKE ROCK 'N' ROLL. I LIKE BEING WITH JOHN. BUT I'M NOT REALLY MUCH OF A BASS PLAYER.
I GUESS I'M ONLY IN THE BAND COZ OF JOHN ...

I THOUGHT I COULD EARN SOME MONEY AND HAVE SOME FUN TRAVELING AROUND EUROPE.
I NEVER THOUGHT IT'D BE SUCH HARD WORK. DAY IN, DAY OUT AND ALL NIGHT LONG.

OH, WAIT ...
THIS IS A GOOD PLACE.

CAN YOU PLEASE ... TAKE YOUR SUNGLASSES ...
AND MY ... MY ...
YOUR SCARF?
YES. THANK YOU.

»Love me tender«

November 1960

I'VE GOT ANOTHER IDEA FOR A SERIES OF PORTRAITS.
WE'RE GOING TO MEET AGAIN ON MONDAY.

I HOPE THE WEATHER DOESN'T GET WORSE.

MMH ...

ANYWAY. TELL ME ...
HOW WAS IT AT YOUR PARENTS' IN BERLIN?
OH, LIKE ALWAYS.

ASTRID ...
YOU'D HAVE TO BE BLIND NOT TO SEE IT.
WHAT?

THE FIRST TIME I TALKED TO HIM, STUART WAS ASKING ABOUT YOU.
HE WANTED TO KNOW EVERYTHING ABOUT YOU.

IT'S SO ... OBVIOUS ... WHAT'S BETWEEN YOU TWO.
IT'S SIMPLY UNAVOIDABLE.

I MEAN ...
IT'S LONG SINCE HAPPENED, HASN'T IT?

YES.

AND,
ARE YOU ...?
NO.
I ALREADY
KNEW.
AND I'M
HAPPY FOR
YOU BOTH.
I MEAN,
WHAT ELSE
CAN I SAY?
AFTER ALL,
I WANT YOU TO
BE HAPPY.
AND YOU
TWO ARE SIMPLY
MADE FOR EACH
OTHER.

LOVE ME TENDER...
LOVE ME SWEET...
NEVER LET ME GO...
YOU HAVE MADE MY LIFE COMPLETE...
AND I LOVE YOU SO...
LOVE ME TENDER...

LOVE ME TRUE...
ALL MY DREAMS FULFILL...
FOR, MY DARLING...
I LOVE YOU...
AND I ALWAYS WILL...

YOU'VE GOT TO COME AND SEE HIM PLAY, KLAUS.

HE'S FANTASTIC. A REALLY GOOD SINGER ...
AND THE BEST GUITAR PLAYER I'VE EVER MET.

WHO ARE THEY TALKING ABOUT?

TONY SHERIDAN.
THEY PLAYED WITH HIM AT THE TOP TEN ON THE REEPERBAHN.

AND JOHN'S ALREADY TALKED TO THE CLUB OWNER.
THEY MIGHT BE ABLE TO START PLAYING THERE.
YEAH, PLAYING THE TOP TEN WOULD BE SO SOUND.
BETTER THAN THIS HOLE.
THE BEST THING ABOUT IT IS ...
WE WOULDN'T HAVE TO SLEEP IN THOSE BUNKS AT THE OLD CINEMA ANY MORE.
ECKHORN'S OFFERED US A ROOM IN HIS FLAT ABOVE THE CLUB.
WE'D HAVE WARM QUILTS, A HEATER, AND A PROPER BATHROOM.
WHAT ABOUT FRY-UPS? THEY SERVE THEM TOO?

SO WHAT ARE WE WAITING FOR?

HAVE YOU READ OUR CONTRACTS?
WE CAN'T JUST START PLAYING SOMEWHERE ELSE. WE'VE GOT A DEAL WITH THAT KOSCHMIDER BLOKE ...

WE'RE PRACTICALLY HIS SLAVES. I THINK HE ACTUALLY OWNS US ...

COME ON, WHO CARES ABOUT KOSCHMIDER AND HIS CONTRACTS? WE'RE NOBODY'S SLAVES. RIGHT?
ONE DAY WE'LL BE THE ONES WRITING UP THE CONTRACTS! JUST WAIT TILL WE'RE AS BIG AS THE SHADOWS!

THE SHADOWS? FUCK THAT!
I WANNA BE AS BIG AS ELVIS!

WHAT THE ... OH, NO! NOT AGAIN!
HEY! THAT'S ENOUGH! OUT WITH YA!
I HATE THIS PLACE.
LET'S GET OUT OF HERE.
ASTRID?
STU?

ANGST ...
THAT'S A
STRANGE
WORD.

YES,
BUT ...
AN- ANXIETY?
I CAN'T SAY
IT ...

I WISH MY ENGLISH WAS BETTER ... I WANT TO LEARN. I HAVE TO...
I TRIED TO READ A BOOK IN ENGLISH ... BY OSCAR WILDE. I WANT TO UNDERSTAND, BUT ...
WHEN YOU SPEAK WITH JOHN, I DON'T UNDERSTAND A WORD ... I HATE IT.
WE'RE JUST TALKING RUBBISH ... YOU SHOULDN'T LEARN ENGLISH FROM US.
YOU'RE SMARTER THAN ME. AND YOU'RE EAGER TO LEARN.
I UNDERSTAND YOU GOOD ... NO ... FINE.
MAYBE MY GERMAN WILL GET BETTER. BUT IT'S A TOUGH LANGUAGE.

AND HE'S ALSO AN ARTIST?

YES. HE RECENTLY SOLD HIS FIRST PICTURE.

I'VE ONLY SEEN SKETCHES HE'S DRAWN IN HIS SKETCH BOOK. HE'S TALENTED ...
... AND INTELLIGENT — AT LEAST, AS FAR AS I CAN UNDERSTAND HIM.

NOW I KNOW WHY YOU WERE SO KEEN TO GO TO THAT CELLAR BAR EVERY NIGHT.

YEAH, THERE REALLY WAS A SPARK BETWEEN US FROM THE MOMENT WE MET ... IT'S DIFFICULT TO DESCRIBE.
YOU THINK IT'S ALL TOO FAST, DON'T YOU?

NO. WHAT AM I SUPPOSED TO SAY? THAT YOU SHOULD KEEP A LEVEL HEAD?

I CAN'T. AND MY HEART TELLS ME THAT I'M DOING THE RIGHT THING.

GOOD.
I'VE GOT A GOOD FEELING ABOUT HIM, TOO. I LIKE HIM ... A LOT.

I DON'T EXACTLY KNOW WHAT IS GOING ON ...

CAFE
YOU KNOW GEORGE IS ONLY SEVENTEEN ...
HE'S NOT OLD ENOUGH TO BE OUT AFTER TEN, LET ALONE PLAY AT CLUBS!
THE POLICE HAVE FOUND OUT HE'S UNDERAGE AND HE HAS TO GO BACK TO LIVERPOOL.
GOD KNOWS HOW WE'RE SUPPOSED TO PLAY WITHOUT HIM.
JOHN'LL HAVE TO PLAY HIS PARTS ON LEAD, BUT ... IT WON'T BE THE SAME.
AND THEN THERE'S OUR MANAGER ...
KOSCHMIDER?
Leder
YEAH. HE'S ALREADY WELL PISSED OFF WITH US.
HE KNOWS WE WANNA PLAY THE TOP TEN.

BUT ... WELL, WE SIGNED THAT STUPID CONTRACT WITH HIM.
IT STOPS US FROM PLAYING ANYWHERE ELSE IN THIS PART OF TOWN.

MON
BUT YOU PLAYED WITH SHERIDAN AT THE TOP TEN ...

YEAH, AND KOSCHMIDER SEEMS TO KNOW.
AND ALL OF A SUDDEN, GEORGE IS BEING SENT HOME ... THE REST OF US HAVE TO LEAVE BY THE END OF NOVEMBER ANYWAY.

NOVEMBER? NO ...

LOVE ME TENDER...
LOVE ME LONG...
TAKE ME TO YOUR HEART...

FOR IT'S THERE THAT I BELONG...
AND WE'LL NEVER PART...

ASTRID?
WE FELL ASLEEP. IT'S LATE. I HAVE TO GO.

PLEASE STAY WITH ME ... NOT AT THE THEATER.

ARE YOU CARRYING HALF OF HAMBURG BACK WITH YOU?
WELL, I COULDN'T LEAVE MY NEW AMP BEHIND, COULD I?
I HAVE TO TRY AND KEEP IT ALL TOGETHER.

OH GOD, YOU'RE GOING TO HAVE A LONG TRIP.
GEORGE! YOUR TRAIN!

THANKS, STU, MATE ... I'LL BE ALL RIGHT. DON'T YOU WORRY.
I JUST HOPE I DON'T MISS THE LAST FERRY FROM HOLLAND.

YOU GOT ENOUGH MONEY FOR THE TRAIN BACK TO LIVERPOOL?

YEAH. I'LL BE ALL RIGHT WITH WHAT I GOT SAVED.

GEORGE!
GEORGE!

KLAUS!

PLEASE DON'T FORGET TO WRITE ME A LETTER!
HEAR ME?

I WON'T FORGET YOU!
STUART! LOOK AFTER THEM, WILL YOU?

WILL DO.

SEE YOU IN LIVERPOOL!

Bahnsteig
4
YEAH, SEE YOU SOON!

BON VOYAGE!

POOR KID ... SAFE TRIP, MATE.

BAR
BIER
THAT'S IT.

HOTEL
TONIGHT WAS OUR LAST GIG AT THAT FUCKIN' KAISERKELLER.

BUT WHAT WAS KOSCHMIDER SO WORKED UP ABOUT?
WHAT WAS HE YELLING AT YOU?

I DON'T GIVE A SHIT.
WE'LL GET OUR BAGS AND MOVE INTO THE TOP TEN STRAIGHT AWAY.

WINTERHUDER
PILS
Becks
keller
Das in
WELL, STU'S ALREADY MOVED OUT ...
THE LUCKY SOD.

YEAH, AND I'M GLAD YOU'RE GETTING OUT OF THAT DUMP, TOO.

AT LAST!
ECKHORN SAYS HE PAYS MORE THAN THIRTY MARKS A NIGHT ... FOR EVERYONE IN THE BAND.

THERE YOU ARE! YOU SAY GOODBYE TO KOSCHMIDER?

LET'S GET A PINT AND DRINK TO OUR BRIGHT FUTURE!

SORRY, MATE, I'VE GOT OTHER THINGS TO DO ...
SEE YOU TOMORROW AT THE TOP TEN!

OTEL
DON'T YOU WANT TO GO WITH THEM?
NAH, NOT TONIGHT.

WHERE ARE WE GOING?
HH-CY 268

BIER
bi Erich
THERE'S SOMETHING I WANNA SHOW YOU ...

ERNST
YOU KNOW I WANNA STAY WITH YOU, RIGHT?

I MEAN FOREVER ... WE AGREE ON THAT, RIGHT?

ARE YOU CRAZY, STUART?

NO, I'M IN LOVE ...

... BUT MAYBE THAT'S THE SAME THING.

WHAT'S HE TALKING ABOUT?

YEAH, THE POLICE ARE LOOKING FOR US.
THE POLICE?
I DON'T KNOW WHAT IT'S ABOUT. PAUL AND PETE HAVE ALREADY BEEN ARRESTED.

AND I'VE GOT NO IDEA WHERE JOHN IS.

WE'LL GO TO THE REEPERBAHN POLICE STATION FIRST.
I'LL CALL YOU.

WHERE CAN JOHN BE? HE'S ALREADY MOVED OUT OF THE BAMBI CINEMA ...
... AND STUART WAS ALREADY AT THE TOP TEN.

YEAH, THE POLICE, TOO ... AND THEY'RE SUPPOSED TO BE PLAYING THERE TONIGHT.

... MAYBE JOHN DOESN'T EVEN KNOW THEY'RE LOOKING FOR HIM.

YOU WON'T FIND JOHN.
YOU MIGHT AS WELL WAIT HERE. MAYBE HE'LL SHOW UP.

OKAY. SEE YOU LATER.

POLIZEI
... I DON'T UNDERSTAND WHY IT'S TAKING SO LONG. I ALREADY GAVE ALL THIS INFORMATION THIS MORNING ...
YOU CAN WAIT UPSTAIRS. SOMEONE WILL CALL YOU SOON.

FRÄULEIN
KIRCHHERR?

GOOD EVENING.
GOOD EVENING.

WE'RE INVESTIGATING ACCUSATIONS OF ... ARSON AT ... PAUL-ROOSENSTRASSE 33.

BUT YOU'RE ... HERR SUTCLIFFE DOESN'T EVEN LIVE THERE ANYMORE.
YES, HE SAID THAT AND GAVE THIS ADDRESS ...
HE LIVES WITH ME. WE'RE ENGAGED AND ...
IS IT YOUR ADDRESS?

YES, THAT'S ...
YOUR ID CARD PLEASE ...

THANK YOU. WE STILL NEED TO CHECK THE GENTLEMEN'S RESIDENCE PERMITS.
AND, OF COURSE, THEIR WORK PERMITS.

WE MAY LEAVE.
ASTRID!

WE DIDN'T SET FIRE TO THE DIGS!
WHAT DID THEY SAY?
MAYBE WE ACCIDENTALLY, LIKE, SINGED A BIT OF THE WALL, BUT ...

PETE AND ME JUST NEEDED SOME LIGHT WHILE WE WERE PACKING. SO WE LIT A MATCH AND ...

I TOLD THEM I DIDN'T HAVE ANYTHING TO DO WITH IT.
BUT I GUESS THIS IS ALL THANKS TO KOSCHMIDER.

EVERYTHING IS ALL RIGHT.
NOTHING HAPPENED. LET'S GO.

Hofbräu

TOP TEN CLUB

Steak-house

HOLSTEN

MAN! I'M DRIPPING WITH SWEAT! WHAT D'YA THINK OF THE GIG?

ECKHORN SAYS HE JUST NEEDS TO SORT OUT OUR IMMIGRATION PROBLEMS AND THEN WE CAN SIGN THE CONTRACT.
ISN'T IT GREAT? WE'RE FINALLY GETTING TO PLAY HERE!

YOU SHOULD BE HAPPY THE GESTAPO LET YOU GO ...

JOHN? YOU STILL WORRIED ABOUT WHAT HAPPENED WITH THE POLICE?

IT WAS JUST A FEW GERMANS IN UNIFORMS ...

YOU AND TONY SHERIDAN ARE A PERFECT MATCH!
YOU'RE NOT WRONG THERE, MATE!

CHEERS!
WILLKOMMEN IM TOP TEN!

STUART ...
STU!
WAKE UP!

KLAUS?

NO, BUT PAUL AND PETE HAVE BEEN ARRESTED AND DEPORTED ...
THEY'RE BOTH ALREADY ON A PLANE BACK TO ENGLAND. IT ALL HAPPENED SO FAST.

JOHN'S STILL HERE, YES ...
HE'S JUST BEEN TO THE AUTHORITIES, BUT ...

NONE OF THEM HAVE VALID WORK PERMITS OR ANYTHING.
I MEAN, THEY HAVEN'T ACTUALLY HAD THE PROPER PAPERS SINCE THEY GOT HERE.

PETER ECKHORN PROBABLY PROMISED TO TAKE CARE OF IT ALL SO THAT THEY COULD START PLAYING AS SOON AS POSSIBLE.
YEAH, THAT WOULD BE GREAT.

NO,
I DON'T
KNOW.

IT WAS
PROBABLY
KOSCHMIDER
WHO REPORTED
THEM.

AT THE END
OF THE DAY,
IT DOESN'T
MATTER ...

I DON'T
THINK WE CAN
DO ANYTHING ...

ARE YOU AFRAID TO TELL YOUR MOTHER ABOUT OUR ENGAGEMENT?
NO. IF SHE DOESN'T LIKE YOU, I WON'T GO BACK.

I TALKED TO MY MOTHER ABOUT THE ATTIC. SHE SAID YOU CAN USE IT AS A STUDIO, FOR PAINTING ...
WE ONLY NEED TO GET A FEW THINGS OUT OF THERE AND CLEAN UP A BIT.
THEN YOU CAN START PAINTING AGAIN. WE WILL GET YOU EVERYTHING YOU NEED.
YOU'RE AMAZING, ASTRID!
RIGHT NOW I'M JUST HAPPY BEING HERE WITH YOU. I DON'T NEED MUCH MORE THAN THAT.
OH, THAT'S NOT TRUE. YOU NEED A LOT OF THINGS ...
... CANVAS, PAPER, BRUSHES, PAINT ...

»Paolozzi«

March 1961

FINALLY! IT'S CONFIRMED. BY THE END OF MARCH WE'LL BE PLAYING AT THE TOP TEN!
GOOD NEWS!

ECKHORN GOT WORK PERMITS FOR ALL OF US UNTIL THE FIRST OF JULY.
GEORGE WROTE THAT THEY CAN'T WAIT TO GET BACK HERE.

I'VE FINISHED YOUR TROUSERS. YOU CAN TRY THEM ON.

PERFECT FIT.
I'LL SEE IF I CAN FINISH THE JACKET NEXT WEEK.

I WISH I HAD MORE TIME TO WORK ON YOUR SUIT.
THERE'S SO MUCH WORK AT REINHART'S AT THE MOMENT.

COME ON, IT'S JUST A SUIT ...
IT CAN WAIT ... AND I CAN WAIT.

BESIDES, I DON'T WANT YOU SPENDING YOUR NIGHTS OFF STUCK BEHIND A SEWING MACHINE.

YOU SAID I COULD WEAR YOUR CLOTHES ANYWAY.
THEY'RE NEARLY ALL MY SIZE ...

JA. YOU'RE RIGHT.
AND MOST OF THEM LOOK EVEN BETTER ON YOU.

SO, I GUESS THAT MEANS I CAN BORROW YOUR VELVET SHIRT FOR PETER'S PARTY TONIGHT?

OF COURSE. YOU LOOK GORGEOUS IN IT.

HI ASTRID!

SAY, I HEARD YOU TWO GOT ENGAGED?
I CAN'T BELIEVE ALL THE THINGS I'VE MISSED OUT ON.

SO, IS STUART STILL PLAYING IN THAT ROCK 'N' ROLL BAND?
YEAH. THEY START PLAYING AGAIN AT THE TOP TEN NEXT WEEK.
THAT SOUNDS A LOT BETTER THAN THAT BAR THEY WERE PLAYING IN.
NO ONE DARED TO GO IN THERE ...

THIS TIME THEY'VE ALL GOT RESIDENCE PERMITS TILL THE END OF JUNE.

WELL, THAT SOUNDS PROFESSIONAL.
WEREN'T THEY ACCUSED OF ARSON OR SOMETHING, TOO?

I THINK I DEFINITELY HAVE TO MEET THIS BAND.

BUT HONESTLY, HOW SERIOUS IS STUART ABOUT THE BAND AND ABOUT MUSIC?

WELL, HE'S ALREADY SERIOUSLY PURSUING OTHER THINGS.

HE ALSO WRITES POEMS AND SHORT STORIES ...
BUT THE MAIN THING IS THAT HE'S STARTED PAINTING AGAIN.

WE'VE JUST CONVERTED OUR ATTIC INTO A STUDIO.
NOW STUART'S FINALLY GOT A PLACE TO WORK.

HOW WONDERFUL!
THEN YOU JUST HAVE TO SHOW ME HIS PICTURES.

AH, HERE HE IS!
STUART, I JUST TOLD PETER ABOUT YOU ...
HE'S AN ART STUDENT AT THAT OTHER SCHOOL I MENTIONED.

REMEMBER, I THOUGHT THAT MAYBE THEY ACCEPT GUEST STUDENTS AND ...

OH, OF COURSE! THE TERM HAS ALREADY STARTED, BUT ...
YOU CAN ENROLL AS A GUEST STUDENT ANY TIME.

COME ON OVER BABY ... WHOLE LOTTA SHAKIN' GOIN' ON

I SAID COME ON OVER BABY ...

BABY, YOU CAN'T GO WRONG

WHOLE LOTTA SHAKIN' GOIN' ON

I SPOKE TO THE ASSISTANT DIRECTOR OF THE ART SCHOOL ...

YOU CAN TAKE THREE CLASSES A WEEK AS A GUEST STUDENT.
YOU ONLY NEED TO BRING A FEW DRAWINGS AND ...

JUST SOME SAMPLES OF MY WORK? A PORTFOLIO? WHEN?

WE CAN GO THERE TOMORROW ... WAIT!
GEORGE CALLED FROM THE STATION. THEY'VE ARRIVED!

*HOW ARE YOU, MRS KIRCHHERR?

OF COURSE!
I'M THE HAPPIEST AND LUCKIEST MAN IN TOWN!
I SEE YOU'RE EVEN WEARING HER CLOTHES NOW.
I'M LIVING THE HIGH LIFE! ASTRID'S MA HAS LET ME HAVE THE WHOLE ATTIC TO PAINT IN!
YOU POOR OLD BOHEMIAN ARTISTS ...
SO, YOU'RE NOT MOVING TO PARIS?
NO.
BUT ONLY BECAUSE MY FRENCH IS EVEN WORSE THAN MY GERMAN.
THEN AGAIN ... I'D FOLLOW THIS GIRL ANYWHERE.

... BUT SARTRE AND DE BEAUVOIR AREN'T MARRIED EITHER.

I THINK THEY EVEN LIVE IN SEPARATE APARTMENTS.

BUT WE WANT TO LIVE TOGETHER. MY WORK IS HERE, AND STUART ...
WELL, HE DOESN'T WANT TO LIVE OFF ME.

DOES HE WANT TO GO BACK TO LIVERPOOL?

NO. AND HE DEFINITELY DOESN'T WANT TO GO TO THE COLLEGE THERE.

PERHAPS HE CAN WORK HERE LATER WHEN HIS GERMAN IS BETTER.

IN ANY CASE, FIRST HE WANTS TO APPLY AS A GUEST STUDENT AT LERCHENFELD ART SCHOOL ...

OH, THAT SOUNDS GOOD.
THEY'LL ACCEPT HIM. I KNOW THEY WILL.

YOU THINK
I CAN PAINT
OVER THIS?

OH ...
YOU HAD BETTER
ASK MY MOTHER.
I DON'T KNOW ...

I FOUND
THIS MASTERPIECE
COLLECTING DUST
IN A CORNER UP
THERE.
I THINK
YOU CAN
HAVE IT.

WHAT
ARE YOU
LOOKING
FOR?
I WANNA
TRY OUT A FEW
THINGS ... EXPERIMENT
A BIT ... USE DIFFERENT
MATERIALS, TRY
SOME NEW TOOLS,
YOU KNOW?

I'M JUST
LOOKING FOR
SOMETHING TO
USE INSTEAD OF
THOSE BORING OLD
BRUSHES.

THIS IS PERFECT.

I'LL BUY YOUR MA A NEW ONE.

DON'T YOU NEED A HAIRCUT, TOO?
I HOPE SO. I'M GOING TO MEET KLAUS AND CUT HIS HAIR.
YOU THINK YOU'LL BE BACK BEFORE I LEAVE FOR THE TOP TEN?

I WAS JUST ABOUT TO ASK ...
I THINK IT'S ABOUT TIME FOR A CHANGE.

YES.

HE HE
HA HA
HEE HEE

LOOK AT THE STATE OF YOU!

HE LOOKS JUST LIKE KLAUS, DOESN'T HE?
YEAH. HE'S ONE OF THEM ... AN ARTIST, LIKE.

SHUT IT, WILL YA? I JUST LIKE IT LIKE THIS.

THE BEST THINGS IN LIFE ARE FREE ... BUT YOU CAN KEEP 'EM FOR THE BIRDS AND BEES

NOW GIVE ME MONEY... THAT'S WHAT I WANT...

OH, THERE THEY ARE!
I WAS CURIOUS ... SO, THIS IS WHERE YOU HIDE YOURSELVES EVERY NIGHT.
YEAH, EXCEPT WEEKENDS, WHEN IT'S FULL OF SECRETARIES, RIGHT?
YEAH, YOU COULD SAY THAT.
SO, OF COURSE, I WANTED TO SEE STUART AND THIS BAND, FINALLY.
AND THERE'S NEWS FROM THE COLLEGE. IT SEEMS STUART'S PORTFOLIO HAS GONE OVER VERY WELL ...
I SPOKE TO A PROFESSOR ... STUART MIGHT BE ABLE TO GET A SCHOLARSHIP.

YOU DON'T WANT TO PLAY WITH THE GROUP ANY MORE, DO YOU?
TO BE HONEST, I'D RATHER BE PAINTING ALL DAY AND NIGHT.
I LIKE BEING WITH THE LADS ON STAGE, BUT ...
YOU KNOW, IT'S THESE SEVEN-HOUR SESSIONS DURING THE WEEK, AND EIGHT ON WEEKENDS ...
AND WE ONLY GET ONE FIFTEEN-MINUTE BREAK EVERY HOUR ...
IT PAYS WELL, BUT IT'S HARD WORK.
YOU CAN'T DO IT WITHOUT THE PILLS AND BEER.
I JUST WISH I COULD MAKE A LIVING WITH MY ART ... SOMEDAY.
I NEED TO GET THIS SCHOLARSHIP. I'LL WRITE TO MA AND ASK HER TO SEND ME MY CERTIFICATES AND THINGS.

LOVE ME TENDER...
LOVE ME DEAR...
TELL ME YOU ARE MINE...
I'LL BE YOURS THROUGH ALL THE YEARS...
TILL THE END OF TIME...

OH, THE MEN FROM THE RECORD COMPANY ...
IT LOOKS LIKE THEY'VE BROUGHT CONTRACTS WITH THEM.

JOHN TOLD ME THEY MIGHT BE MAKING A RECORD WITH TONY ...

ALL RIGHT. SEE YOU NEXT WEEK.
I CAN'T BELIEVE IT ...
WHO WAS THE DARK-HAIRED MAN?
THAT WAS EDUARDO PAOLOZZI. HE'S A PROFESSOR AT THE ART SCHOOL.
DO YOU KNOW HIM? I THINK HE'S QUITE FAMOUS. AND IT JUST SO HAPPENS THAT HE'S SCOTTISH!
HE WANTS TO SEE MY WORK. HE MIGHT LET ME INTO HIS CLASS.
HE SAID THAT THEN IT'D BE EASY TO GET A SCHOLARSHIP ...

OHANN BARTELS
ASTRA
BIER
JOHN, I'M FINE WITH IT.
PAUL'S BETTER ON BASS. IT'S JUST A FACT.
WE ALL KNOW THAT.
I DON'T WANT TO EMBARRASS YOU, LIKE, WHEN WE RECORD WITH SHERIDAN.
YOU KNOW HOW PAUL GOES MAD EVERY TIME I PLAY A BUM NOTE ...

I WANNA ENROLL AT THIS ART SCHOOL. TOMORROW I'M GONNA MEET PAOLOZZI, YOU KNOW ...
YEAH, I KNOW WHAT YOU MEAN!
I KNOW IT'S A GREAT CHANCE AND I'M HAPPY FOR YOU ...
... AND I KNOW YOU'D ALMOST GRADUATED BACK HOME WHEN I TALKED YOU INTO BUYING A BASS GUITAR ...
... JOINING A ROCK 'N' ROLL BAND AND COMING TO PLAY IN NIGHTCLUBS AND FILTHY CELLARS IN HAMBURG ...
ANYWAY, I'M GLAD YOU'VE FOUND WHAT YOU REALLY WANNA DO.
CAN'T SAY THE SAME FOR THAT NEW HAIRCUT, THOUGH.
tter
uben
HOLSTEN EDEL
BUT YOU'RE STILL PART OF THIS BAND!

IT WENT GREAT!

WELL, YOU TWO LOOK HAPPY ...
PAOLOZZI'S ACCEPTED HIM INTO HIS MASTER CLASS!
THAT WAS QUICK! AND THAT MEANS HE'S ALSO GOING TO GET A SCHOLARSHIP?
YEAH, AND THEN HE'LL BE OFFICIALLY ENROLLED.
WE JUST HANDED IN THE APPLICATION.
HE CAN START IN PAOLOZZI'S CLASS TOMORROW.

MY HEAD'S HURTING ... I THINK I'M GONNA STOP FOR THE NIGHT.
THEN COME DOWN AND SIT WITH ME.
COME ON, KLAUS, YOU PLAY ...
OH, I DON'T ...
WELL, I CAN TRY ...
BOM BOM
DOM
BOM DOM

BOM
DOM

ALL RIGHT!
NOT BAD ...

COME
AND PLAY
UP HERE!
YEAH,
COME ON,
KLAUS!

HE'S
MUCH BETTER
THAN ME.

THEY'D
BE FINE
WITHOUT
ME.

ASTRID. YOUR MOTHER'S ON THE PHONE.
SHE SAYS STUART'S NOT WELL ...

YES ... WHERE?
IN PAOLOZZI'S CLASS?

YES, THAT WAS LUCKY ... AND HOW IS HE NOW?
IT WAS PROBABLY JUST HIS CIRCULATION ...

YES, THAT'S FINE.
I'LL TAKE HIM TO DR. HOMMELHOFF'S TOMORROW.

WELL, TO BE HONEST ...
... I'VE NEVER SEEN ANYTHING LIKE IT.
YOU'RE SIMPLY MENTALLY EXHAUSTED ...
THAT NATURALLY EFFECTS YOUR STOMACH ... AND IT'S ALSO THE CAUSE OF YOUR HEADACHES.
PLEASE LAY OFF THE CIGARETTES ... AND ALCOHOL, IF POSSIBLE.
NO CIGARETTES?
PLEASE TELL HIM HE SHOULD SMOKE LESS.
I'LL ALSO PRESCRIBE SOMETHING FOR HIS DIGESTION AND AND BREATHING PROBLEMS.

A GASTRITIS PROBLEM LIKE THIS CAN BE DEALT WITH.
HE SHOULD TAKE THE TABLETS IN THE MORNING. AND HE SHOULD EAT FOOD THAT'S GENTLE ON THE STOMACH ... AND REST AFTER EATING.

IF YOU CONTINUE TO HAVE PROBLEMS ...
WE'LL HAVE TO CONSIDER REMOVING THE APPENDIX.

OTHERWISE, I DON'T SEE ANY REASON TO WORRY.
OH YES, AND DON'T FORGET TO PICK UP THE ADDRESS OF THE MASSAGE PRACTICE ON YOUR WAY OUT.

A COUPLE OF SESSIONS AND THE STRESS AND HEADACHES SHOULD DISAPPEAR.

Milch
HE SAID IT'S NOTHING TO WORRY ABOUT?

NO, IT'S NOTHING SERIOUS.

YES, IT'S PROBABLY JUST HIS NERVES AND STOMACH ... I MEAN, HE'S SO THIN.

BUT PLAYING WITH THE BAND EVERY NIGHT ...
... AND NOW GOING TO COLLEGE EVERY DAY, PLUS THE WORK HE DOES HERE ...

PERHAPS IT'S ALL JUST TOO MUCH, DON'T YOU BOTH THINK?

BUT AFTER THEY'VE RECORDED WITH SHERIDAN THEY'VE ONLY GOT ANOTHER WEEK PLAYING THE TOP TEN.
HE'LL STOP THEN. THAT'S WHAT HE WAS PLANNING ANYWAY.

WE DID FOUR TRACKS BACKING SHERIDAN AND TOMORROW WE MIGHT LAY DOWN THAT JIMMY REED NUMBER.

DID YOU GET TO RECORD SOMETHING ON YOUR OWN ... WITHOUT SHERIDAN?
YEAH, WE DID *AIN'T SHE SWEET* WITH JOHN ON VOCALS. BUT ... I DON'T KNOW, LIKE ...

IT WAS STRANGE BEING IN A STUDIO. BUT AT LEAST WE GOT TO PLAY TOGETHER AS A BAND, NOT SEPARATELY.
BUT THE SOUND WAS CRAP, JUST THE SAME.

IT JUST AIN'T THE SAME AS PLAYING ON STAGE.
IT SEEMS IMPOSSIBLE TO GET THAT LIVE SOUND DOWN ON TAPE.

THEY'RE GONNA RELEASE *MY BONNIE* IN GERMANY, ANYWAY. THAT'S SAYING SOMETHING!

BUT THAT'S GREAT! YOUR FIRST RECORD!
I CAN'T WAIT TO GO INTO A RECORD SHOP AND BUY IT!

DID YOU SPEAK TO JOHN?
ABOUT ME LEAVING THE BAND?
NO, ABOUT YOUR HEALTH ...
NO, WHY?
I'M FINE.

...on Tabak
OOH! KEEP THAT FISH AWAY FROM ME, WILL YA, GEORGE!

COME ON, WILL YA! I CAN'T STAND THE SMELL ... WHAT TIME IS IT?

ANYONE KNOW WHEN WE GOTTA BE AT THE STATION?

UM ... I DUNNO ...

I THINK THE TRAIN LEAVES ABOUT NOON ... WE'D BETTER GET GOING.

WE'VE GOT 'EM COMIN' OUT OF OUR EARS. I GUESS IT GOT A LITTLE OUT OF HAND.

YOU CAN SAY THAT AGAIN! YOU DIDN'T STOP TALKING ALL NIGHT ...

THAT GOES FOR ALL OF US.
WELL, IT WAS OUR LAST NIGHT ... TOMORROW WE'LL BE BACK IN LIVERPOOL.

CHRIST, YEAH ... WE MIGHT NEVER SEE EACH OTHER AGAIN ...

I ALWAYS GET A BIT SENTIMENTAL WHEN I'M DRUNK.

I GOTTA ADMIT, IT FEELS WEIRD KNOWING STU'S GONNA STAY HERE.
I KNOW HE'S HAPPY AN' ALL WITH ASTRID, BUT ... I'D HAVE LIKED TO HAVE SEEN HIM IN THE BAND.
HE'S JUST DRAWN TO YOUR WORLD. HE PROBABLY BELONGS HERE ...
WELL, YOU KNOW ... I WANT TO PLAY BASS AND ... I WOULD ...
... I WOULD REALLY LIKE TO BE IN THE GROUP.
OH, I'M SORRY, KLAUS.
WE ALREADY DECIDED THAT PAUL'S GONNA PLAY BASS.
DO
HE JUST BOUGHT A NEW GUITAR.

»Stay like that ...«

October 1961

I'M SO HAPPY THOSE LONG NIGHTS PLAYING WITH THE BAND ARE OVER.
I'M SURE HE WAS JUST MENTALLY EXHAUSTED. LIKE DR. HOMMELHOFF SAID.
YEAH, HE'S DOING MUCH BETTER NOW. HE'S EVEN PUT ON SOME WEIGHT.
IT'S JUST THESE HEADACHES THAT HE STILL HAS SOMETIMES.
OFTEN, HE PAINTS LIKE HE'S IN A FRENZY, THE WHOLE NIGHT ... BUT I DON'T THINK HE CAN DO IT ANY OTHER WAY.
I READ THAT NUREYEV, THE BALLET DANCER, IS COMING TO HAMBURG.
I'M GOING TO GET TICKETS FOR YOU TWO. YOU SHOULD ENJOY A NIGHT OUT TOGETHER.

AH, STUART! HELLO!
HOW ARE YOU?
I ONLY CAME TO PICK UP ASTRID ...
BUT I SEE YOU'RE STILL BUSY. I'LL ...
WE'LL BE DONE IN A FEW MINUTES. WE HAVE TO PREPARE EVERYTHING FOR TOMORROW'S SHOOT.
I'LL WAIT, THEN.
STUART, MAY I TAKE A LOOK AT YOUR PICTURES?
I REALLY LIKED THE ONES YOU SHOWED US LAST TIME.
WELL, THEY'RE JUST DRAWINGS ... JUST SKETCHES.

YOU COULD ACTUALLY HELP ME WITH THIS, STUART.
I NEED YOU AS A MODEL FOR THE LIGHT TEST SHOTS.

TURN YOUR HEAD TOWARD ME ...
YES, THAT'S PERFECT.

YOU HAVE IMPROVED, STUART. THESE ARE REALLY GOOD.

ROLLEICORD
OKAY, STAY LIKE THAT ...
CLICK

I CAN'T BELIEVE HE WANTS TO BUY THESE PICTURES FROM ME.
YOU KNOW REINHART — HE WOULDN'T DO THAT.
HE'S NOT JUST TRYING TO BE NICE, IS HE?
HE NEVER SAYS SOMETHING WITHOUT MEANING IT.

KLAUS. HOW MANY COPIES OF THIS DID YOU BUY? ARE ALL OF THEM FOR US?
TONY SHERIDAN
My Bonnie
TONY SHERIDAN AND THE ... BEAT BROTHERS?
YEAH, JOHN SAID THE PRODUCER DIDN'T LIKE THEIR NAME ...

HE SAID *THE BEATLES* SOUNDS TOO MUCH LIKE GERMAN SLANG ... LIKE A WORD FOR PENIS OR SOMETHING LIKE THAT.
I GUESS, IN THE END, THEY DIDN'T CARE. THEY WERE JUST HAPPY TO GET THE CHANCE TO MAKE A RECORD WITH SHERIDAN.
I'LL SEND A FEW COPIES BACK TO LIVERPOOL. I KNOW THEY'RE WAITING FOR THEM.

PLEASE TELL THEM HOW MUCH WE MISS THEM! AND HOW WONDERFUL THEIR FIRST SINGLE IS!
HA HA! YEAH, I WILL.

OH, STU, HERE'S A LETTER FOR YOU FROM THE ART SCHOOL ...
WE'LL HAVE TO REPLY TO GEORGE'S LAST LETTER, ANYWAY.

LET ME SEE ... IT SAYS ...
YOUR SCHOLARSHIP WAS INCREASED BY A FURTHER ONE HUNDRED MARKS!

REALLY? THAT'S EVEN BETTER THAN A RECORD WITH SHERIDAN!

I HEARD HE'S SAID TO BE ONE OF PAOLOZZI'S BEST STUDENTS.
DID YOU EXPECT ANYTHING ELSE?

STUART? I'M BACK!
I'M SORRY IT GOT SO LATE TODAY.
HAVE YOU FINISHED YOUR PAINTING? CAN I SEE IT?
I ONLY NEED TO LOOK AT YOU TO KNOW WHAT YOU THINK.
MAYBE I SHOULD USE MORE BLACK ...
YOU DON'T HAVE TO ... USE MY FAVORITE COLOR TO ...
... JUST TO PLEASE ME.

BUT I DO LIKE TO PLEASE YOU, YOU KNOW?
I KNOW. IT WAS JUST AN IDEA.
I'M STILL LEARNING ... I HAVE TO TRY ALL KINDS OF THINGS OUT.
THERE'S SO MUCH IN MY HEAD ... THINGS I NEED TO MAKE CONCRETE.
I'M TIRED ... I'LL HAVE TO GET UP EARLY AGAIN.
HOW LONG ARE YOU GOING TO BE PAINTING TONIGHT?
I JUST NEED ANOTHER HOUR, MAYBE ...

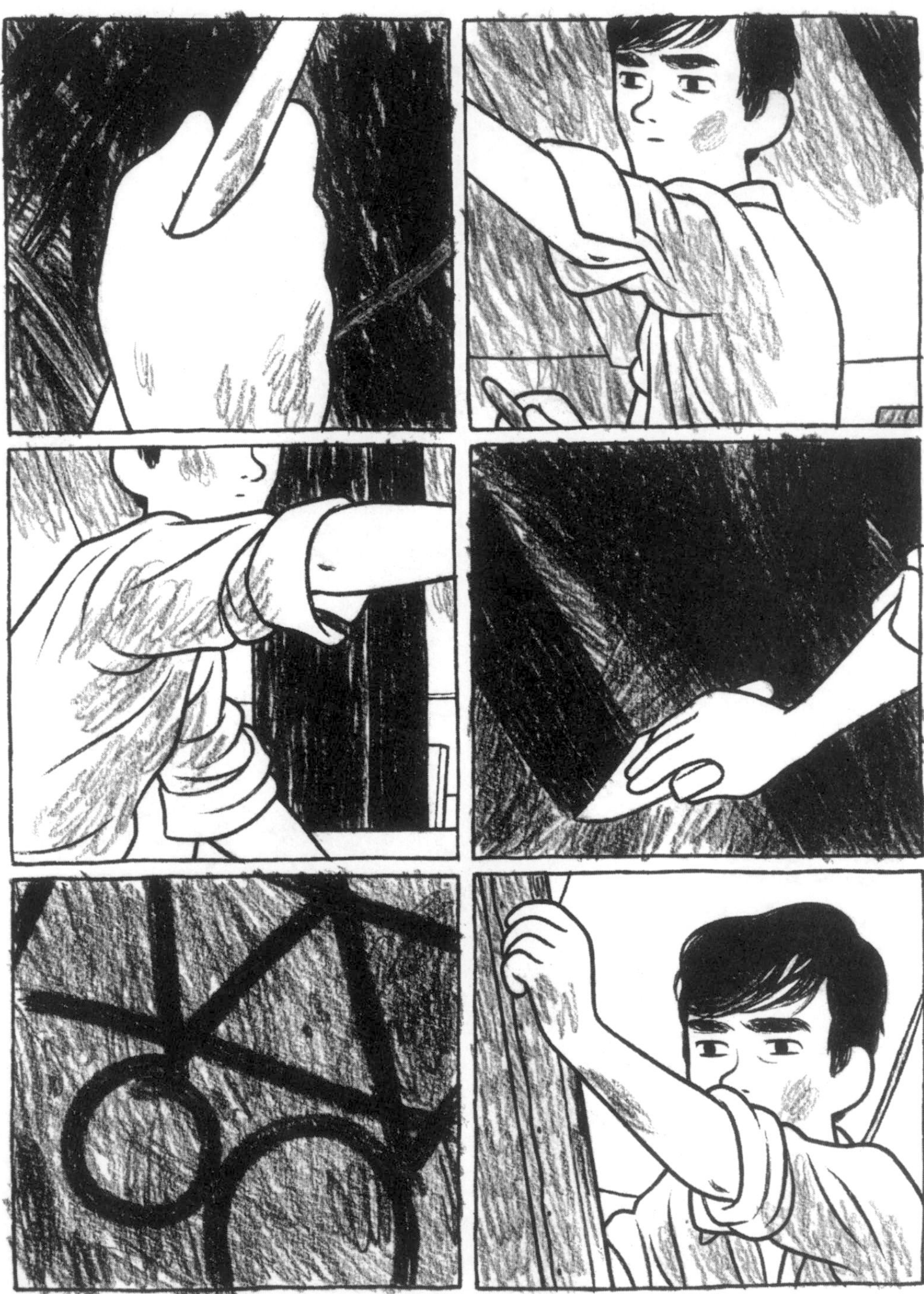

PLEASE, COME TO BED ...

OOH, IT'S TURNED SO COLD AGAIN ...
ARE YOU TAKING STUART FOR HIS MASSAGE TODAY?
YES, WE'RE GOING INTO TOWN THIS AFTERNOON.
HE WANTS TO GET PAINTS AND PAPER, TOO.
HE WORKED LATE LAST NIGHT. I THINK HE'S WORKING ON FIVE PAINTINGS AT THE SAME TIME.

DID YOU KNOW REINHART'S THINKING ABOUT BUYING SOME OF STUART'S PICTURES?
AND HIS PROFESSOR'S ALSO PLEASED WITH HIS WORK.
PLUS, HE UNDERSTANDS THAT STUART CAN OFTEN WORK BETTER HERE.
SOMETIMES I ENVY HIS ENERGY. HE'S ALWAYS TRYING NEW THINGS ...
AND HE'S NEVER COMPLACENT ...
... HE NEVER SAYS, "NOW I'M FINISHED" OR "NOW IT'S GOOD ENOUGH."
TELL ME, IS HE STILL TAKING HIS PILLS DURING THE DAY?
YES, AND HE EATS HIS MILK SOUP AND SLEEPS AN HOUR AFTERWARDS ...
HE'S ALSO SMOKING MUCH LESS. JUST A COUPLE OF CIGARETTES A DAY.

I EVEN MANAGED TO FIND AN ENGLISH TRANSLATION OF THAT BAUDELAIRE BOOK.
OH, THANKS.

NSTRASSE
WELL, YOU KNOW IT REALLY SHOULD BE READ IN THE ORIGINAL FRENCH.
BUT I GUESS, UNLIKE US, STUART CAN READ OSCAR WILDE IN THE ORIGINAL LANGUAGE.

YEAH, I'VE BEEN TRYING THE WILDE AGAIN. IT'S A BIT EASIER THIS TIME.
IS STUART SPEAKING MORE GERMAN NOW?

NO, NOT REALLY. BUT HE COULD SPEAK OLD SIBERIAN ...
... AND I'D STILL LOVE HIM.

GEORGE WRITES THAT THEIR RECORD IS REALLY POPULAR IN CLUBS.

HE WANTS US TO SEND HIM MORE COPIES.
HE'S EVEN SENT MONEY FOR THEM ...

I KNEW IT!
IT CAN'T BE MUCH LONGER NOW TILL TONY SHERIDAN'S LP COMES OUT, DON'T YOU THINK?

I ALREADY SENT THE RECORD COMPANY MY PHOTOS FOR THE COVER. WE'LL SEE ...

YOU HAVEN'T SHOWN ME THOSE PICTURES!
CAN I SEE THEM? HAVE YOU GOT THEM HERE?

OH, I'M NOT PARTICULARLY HAPPY WITH THEM ... IT WAS JUST A PAYING JOB.

I HAD TO SHOOT IN COLOR. THE RECORD COMPANY HAS THE LAST SAY.
WELL, THEN I HOPE THEY PAID WELL!

YEAH. THE MONEY WILL CERTAINLY COME IN HANDY, ESPECIALLY AS WE'RE GOING TO PARIS NEXT YEAR.
WE WANT TO STAY THERE A LITTLE WHILE.

STUART WANTS TO TAKE AS MANY PAINTINGS WITH HIM AS POSSIBLE AND INTRODUCE HIMSELF TO A COUPLE OF GALLERIES.

SO, WE'RE STARTING TO SAVE UP SOME MONEY ...
... STUART'S SELLING HIS GUITAR.

YOU'RE SELLING YOUR BASS?

YEAH, I JUST WANT TO GET RID OF IT.
THERE'S THIS SHOP WHERE PAUL BOUGHT HIS BASS. MAYBE I CAN GET A GOOD PRICE FOR IT THERE.

NO, PLEASE DON'T SELL IT, STUART! I'D LIKE TO HAVE IT.

OH, RIGHT. SURE THING. IT'S YOURS.
NO, NO, WAIT ... I WANT TO PAY FOR IT! SELL IT TO ME!

ASTRID, WHAT DO YOU THINK THE BASS IS WORTH? TWO HUNDRED MARKS?

I DON'T WANT YOUR MONEY. I'LL GIVE IT TO YOU AS A PRESENT.
MAYBE FOR CHRISTMAS ...

NO ... I'LL BUY IT OFF YOU, STUART! NO ARGUMENTS!

CAN YOU IMAGINE? THEY DIDN'T WANT HIM TO LEAVE THE COUNTRY WITH THE BALLET COMPANY!
WELL, THEY DID BUILD A WALL RIGHT THROUGH BERLIN ...
SO THIS IS HIS FIRST TOUR IN THE WEST?
I'VE READ THAT HE REFUSED TO GO BACK TO RUSSIA — HE JUST STAYED IN PARIS.
AREN'T WE LUCKY WE MET ON THIS SIDE OF THE WALL? WE'RE FREE TO GO WHEREVER WE WANT.
WE COULD EVEN GET MARRIED IN PARIS AND GO ON OUR HONEYMOON IN FRANCE. WE COULD GO NEXT YEAR IN JUNE, WHEN I FINISH MY COURSE ...

TOMORROW WE'LL HAVE BEEN ENGAGED FOR EXACTLY ONE YEAR.
THAT'S RIGHT. WE HAVE TO CELEBRATE OUR ANNIVERSARY SOMEHOW.
WE COULD GO TO THAT RESTAURANT WE WENT TO WITH YOUR MA.
AND THIS TIME WE'LL PAY FOR HER. SHE'S ALWAYS BEEN SO GOOD TO ME.
I KNOW THIS SOUNDS SOPPY, BUT I DON'T REGRET A SINGLE DAY I'VE SPENT WITH YOU ...
... IN THIS WET GERMAN CITY.

»Maybe it's too dark«

February 1962

ASTRID! YOU LOOK GORGEOUS. MY GOODNESS!
OH! THANK YOU!
HAVE YOU SEEN KLAUS AROUND?

YES, ON THE SECOND FLOOR. THEY WERE PLAYING JAZZ UP THERE ...
... BUT THEN A DANCE BAND TURNED UP AND EVERYONE WENT CRAZY.
THAT'S RIGHT. I JUST SAW STUART AND KLAUS DANCING.
AND? WHO CUT THE FINER FIGURE?
OH, NEITHER IS UNTALENTED.
BUT, OF COURSE, STUART'S THE ONE DRAWING ALL THE ATTENTION AGAIN.
HE DOES THAT EVEN WHEN HE'S NOT DOING ANYTHING. IT'S NOT JUST PAOLOZZI WITH WHOM HE'S EXCEPTIONALLY ... POPULAR, HERE AT COLLEGE.
ESPECIALLY AFTER ASTRID GAVE HIM THAT HAIRCUT.
PETER, THEY'RE ENGAGED.
OH, I KNOW. I'VE ALREADY CONGRATULATED ASTRID UMPTEEN TIMES ON HER CATCH.

AH, THERE'S KLAUS!

HEY, HAVE YOU HEARD ABOUT THAT NEW CLUB ON THE GROSSE FREIHEIT?
I HEARD IT'S GOING TO BE OPENING IN APRIL ... IN THE OLD STERN CINEMA.

OH, THAT'S BEEN EMPTY FOR AGES, HASN'T IT?
YEAH, BUT NOW THEY'RE GOING TO TURN IT INTO A HUGE ROCK CLUB WITH LIVE MUSIC.

AND THE BEATLES ARE BILLED TO PLAY ON THE OPENING NIGHT.

OH, WHERE EXACTLY HAS STUART GONE TO?
HE WAS STILL DANCING A MOMENT AGO ...

I'M SORRY. RIGHT NOW THERE'S NOTHING MORE I CAN SAY.
IT SEEMS TO HAVE BEEN AN ACUTE ATTACK.
FOR THE TIME BEING, HE NEEDS TO AVOID ANY KIND OF STRESS OR STRAIN ...
HE SHOULD TAKE IT EASY UNTIL THE END OF THE MONTH.
AND HE SHOULD KEEP TAKING THE STOMACH PILLS.

... AND HE HASN'T HAD ANY OTHER ATTACKS LIKE THIS RECENTLY?
NO, NO ...
NOT SINCE LAST AUTUMN. AND HE'S BEEN TAKING HIS MEDICINE REGULARLY.
I THINK THE MASSAGES HAVE ALSO HELPED HIM. GENERALLY HE'S BEEN FINE ...
... EXCEPT FOR THE HEADACHES.
I'LL CONSULT WITH A COLLEAGUE OF MINE AGAIN ...
... WE'LL FIND OUT THE CAUSE OF THIS.

GOOD MORNING, MY DEAR. HOW ARE YOU?

THERE'S A LETTER FROM YOUR FAMILY.

STU, MAYBE YOU SHOULD STAY IN BED IF ...

I'M ALL RIGHT.
I'VE HAD MORE THAN ENOUGH TIME IN BED. I CAN'T STAND IT ANY MORE, BEING SICK ... WHATEVER IT IS THAT'S WRONG WITH ME.

I'M NOT IN ANY PAIN. NO HEADACHES. NOTHING.
SERIOUSLY, I JUST NEED TO PAINT AGAIN.

THAT'S RIGHT. BUT IT'S STILL THERE. YOU SEE THOSE SCRATCHES THROUGH THE LAYERS OF COLOR?
IT LOOKS LIKE YOU'VE MOVED AWAY FROM RED.
IT'S THERE, BENEATH THE BLACK AND SILVER.
MAYBE IT'S TOO DARK. IT NEEDS MORE CONTRAST.
BUT I'M HAPPY WITH THE TEXTURE.
I WAS THINKING ABOUT USING UNMIXED PAINT POWDER. I JUST HAVE TO FIND A WAY TO APPLY IT TO THE CANVAS.
IT'S ALMOST A PAINTED SCULPTURE. BUT THERE'S STILL SO MUCH FURTHER I CAN PUSH IT. IT'S A CONSTANT SEARCH FOR SOMETHING ... ELSE.
I DON'T KNOW. I THINK WHEN IT'S FINISHED THIS PAINTING'S GONNA BE COMPLETELY DIFFERENT FROM ANYTHING I'VE DONE BEFORE.

PETER SAYS HE HASN'T SEEN STUART IN SCHOOL FOR A LONG TIME ...
YEAH, HE'S STILL OUT SICK.
BUT HE'S DOING WELL.

HE'S CONSTANTLY AT HIS EASEL. HE'S NEVER PRODUCED SO MUCH WORK AS HE HAS IN THESE LAST WEEKS ...
I SAW HIS LITHOGRAPHS. I THINK HE JUST KEEPS GETTING BETTER.

I WOULDN'T BE SURPRISED IF I SAW HIS PICTURES HANGING IN PARISIAN GALLERIES SOON ...
YEAH, PARIS. I CAN HARDLY WAIT TO FINALLY GO THERE WITH STUART.

BUT IN APRIL THE BOYS ARE COMING FROM LIVERPOOL ... AND THEN IT'S NOT LONG UNTIL THE EXHIBITION PUT ON BY PAOLOZZI'S MASTER STUDENTS ...
YEAH, SO MAYBE IN JUNE, AFTER THE END OF THE TERM. BUT BEFORE THEN, WE STILL HAVE TO GET MARRIED ...

... IF WE WANT TO BE ABLE TO RENT DOUBLE ROOMS TOGETHER IN PARIS.

... THE BEST THING WOULD BE TO ALSO TAKE A COUPLE OF PROFILE PICTURES OF HER.
RING
RINNG

OH, IT'S YOU ... HI.
NO, I ...

THE MODEL'S GOING IN AN HOUR. WE'LL BE FINISHED THEN.

YES ... BUT I CAN'T. WE'RE NOT FINISHED HERE YET.

OKAY, I'LL SEE YOU LATER.

HE FELL ASLEEP AFTER THE INJECTION ...
OH, I WISH THERE WAS SOMETHING WE COULD DO ...
THIS AFTERNOON HE KEPT TRYING TO GET UP ...
BUT HIS LEGS WOULDN'T HOLD HIM ...
HE WAS DIZZY AND KEPT FEELING FAINT.
DR. HOMMELHOFF SAID TODAY THAT PERHAPS IT'S EPILEPSY AFTER ALL.
HE'S GOING TO CONSULT WITH ANOTHER EXPERT ON IT.

WHEN AT LAST...
MY DREAMS COME TRUE...
DARLING THIS I'LL KNOW...

HAPPINESS WILL FOLLOW YOU...
EVERYWHERE YOU GO...

»What's wrong with you?«

April 1962

YOU LOOK TIRED, ASTRID.
TO TELL YOU THE TRUTH, I'VE BEEN WONDERING WHAT'S UP WITH YOU FOR OVER A WEEK NOW.
OH, I'VE JUST BEEN SLEEPING BADLY.
RING
HOLD ON, I'LL GET IT ...

BUT ...
I ...
YES, I'M ON MY WAY.
...
...
...
...
...

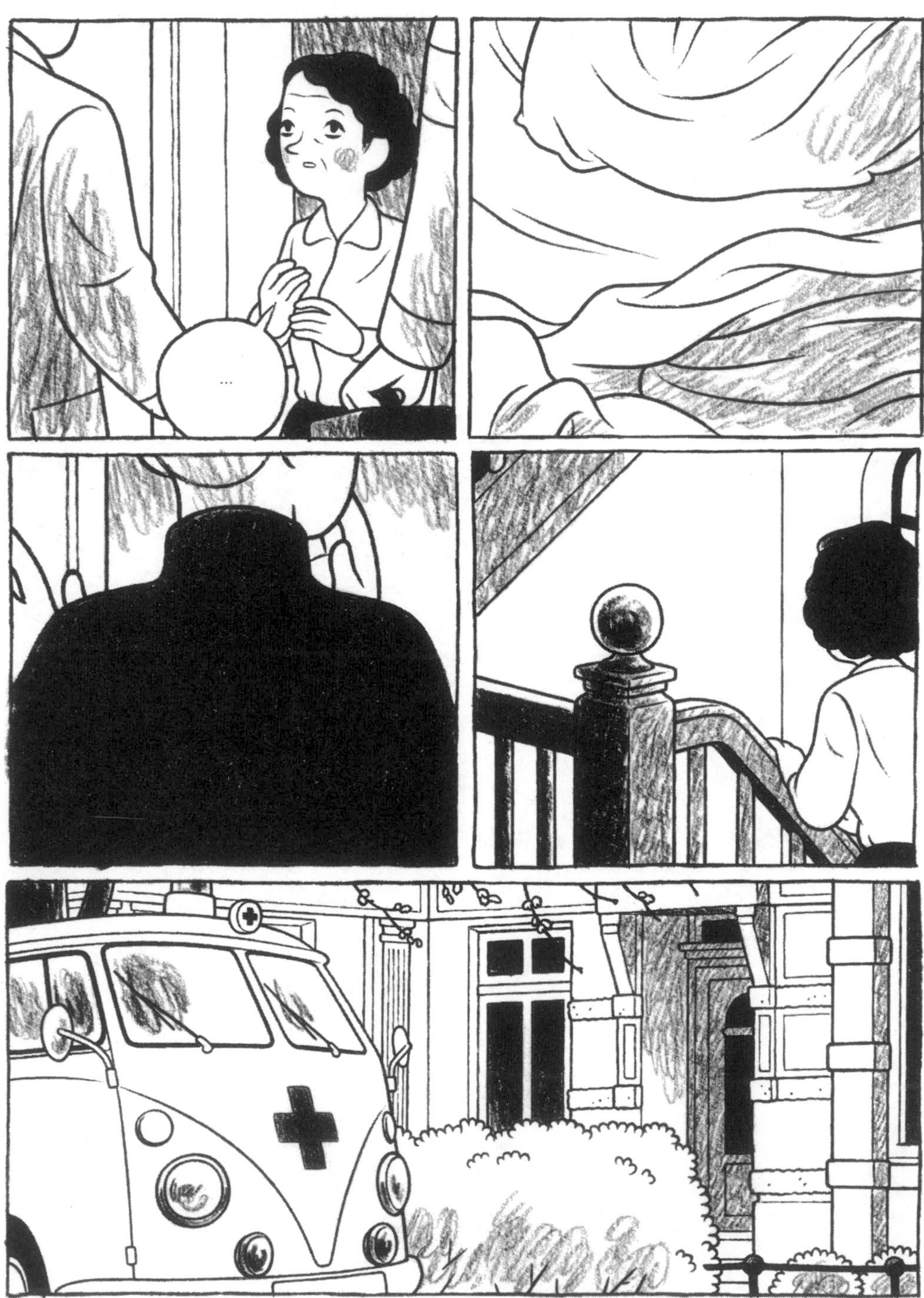

Große Freiheit
Lotto
Star-Club
Rock n' Twist-Parade 1962
Monica
Erotic

HAMBURG
LUFTHANS

ISN'T THAT ASTRID?
YES, THAT'S HER!
ASTRID!

WHAT ARE YOU DOING HERE? WE WERE EXPECTING TO SEE GEORGE ...
YEAH ... HIS PLANE SHOULD ARRIVE IN A MINUTE.

WHAT'S WRONG WITH YOU?

I CAME TO PICK UP STUART'S MOTHER ...
SHE MIGHT BE ON THE SAME PLANE AS GEORGE.

STU'S MOTHER?
BUT WHERE'S STUART?

HEURTEBISE: I'll tell you the secret of all secrets ... Mirrors are doors through which Death comes and goes. Don't tell anyone. So, spend your life looking in the mirror and watch Death at work, like bees in a glass hive.

– Jean Cocteau, *Orpheus*

STUART SUTCLIFFE died on April 10, 1962, from a brain haemorrhage, while en route in an ambulance to a hospital in Hamburg.

The exact cause of his death remains unclear. However, his symptoms and the course of his illness allow us to draw the conclusion that he was born with weak or malformed cerebral vessels (aneurism, angioma), which eventually led to internal bleeding.

Stuart was buried at Huyton Cemetery, Liverpool, in a suit custom-made by Astrid.

ASTRID KIRCHHERR worked until 1963 as an assistant for Reinhart Wolf, and then until 1967 as a freelance photographer. In 1964, she traveled with Max Scheler to England to photograph the filming of The Beatles' *A Hard Day's Night* for *Stern* magazine. However, after that, she turned down the majority of requests for further pictures of The Beatles and avoided public life as much as possible. The reason for this is because she saw herself as a friend of The Beatles and not as the "mop tops'" hairdresser.

Her photos could and can still be seen in numerous international exhibitions, books, and magazines—most recently in a huge retrospective in Liverpool.

Astrid Kirchherr still lives in Hamburg.

KLAUS VOORMANN moved to London in 1963, where he worked in an advertising agency and lived for a while with George Harrison and Ringo Starr. He began his musical career as a bassist in the band Paddy, Klaus & Gibson and was also a member of Manfred Mann and John Lennon's Plastic Ono Band. He also worked as a session musician for, among others, Harry Nilsson, Carly Simon, Randy Newman, Lou Reed, as well as on solo projects by George Harrison, Ringo Starr, and John Lennon.

At the same time, he continued to work as a graphic artist, as he still does. He created the cover for The Beatles' *Revolver* LP as well as the album covers for numerous other artists, such as the Bee Gees, Turbonegro and Trio, whom he also discovered and produced.

He lives with his family near Munich, Germany.

THE BEATLES let Pete Best go in 1962. Together with their new drummer, Ringo Starr, they wrote pop history, before splitting up in 1970 to continue to work on other projects and solo projects. John Lennon was shot in 1980 by a mentally disturbed fan. George Harrison died in 2001 from cancer. Ringo Starr and Paul McCartney, who was knighted in 1997, continue to make music to this day.